WASHING'

JEOPARDY!

Answers and Questions About Our State

by
Carole Marsh

This activity book has material which correlates with the Washington learning standards. At every opportunity, we have tried to relate information to the Washington History and Social Science, English, Science, Math, Civics, Economics, and Computer Technology directives. For additional information, go to our websites: **www.washingtonexperience.com** or **www.gallopade.com**.

GALL◉PADE
INTERNATIONAL

Gallopade is proud to be a member of these educational organizations and associations:

The Washington Experience Series

My First Pocket Guide to Washington!

The Big Washington Reproducible Activity Book

The Washington Coloring Book!

My First Book About Washington!

Washington Jography: A Fun Run Through Our State

The Washington Experience! Sticker Pack

The Washington Experience! Poster/Map

Discover Washington CD-ROM

Washington "GEO" Bingo Game

Washington "HISTO" Bingo Game

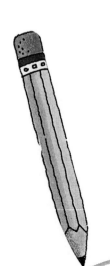

A Word... from the Author

The word is Jeopardy!

I'm sure you've all seen this popular game show. Actually, it's not much different from something kids seem to hate—the good, old-fashioned pop quiz! But how much more fun plain, boring questions and answers are when they're switcherooed into answers and questions!

I'm not trying to copy the actual Jeopardy game show format. I've just tried to use the reverse: "Here's the answer, now what's the question?" formula to make the facts about our state as interesting and intriguing as possible. Also, I think this format is a good double-check to see just how much all that history and geography is registering. Kids often know "facts" only in the memorized-order they learned them, which does not exactly = true knowledge, even if they do pass their tests.

The Answers and Questions on the next pages cover our state's history, geography, people, and much more. You can use the book in a variety of ways. If students want to read it on their own, they'll need to use a sheet of paper to cover the answers, oops!, I mean the questions. You could keep the book on the kitchen table and play Jeopardy while you eat breakfast. In the classroom, you could give the answers orally and let kids give the questions.

Whatever you do, keep score, have fun, let all ages participate, use wrong answers (I mean questions!) as the starting point for improved learning. Let kids have a chance to create their own Jeopardy answers and questions (It's much harder than it looks!). The only thing that should really be put in jeopardy are your frown muscles!

Carole Marsh

Washington Trivia

Answer: Washington's state nickname

QUESTION: What is the Evergreen State?

Answer: Washington's state bird

QUESTION: What is the willow goldfinch?

Answer: Washington's state fish

QUESTION: What is the steelhead trout?

Answer: Washington's state colors

QUESTION: What are green and gold?

Answer: Washington's state tree

QUESTION: What is the western hemlock?

Washington
All Around Our State

Answer: State that borders Washington to the south

QUESTION: What is Oregon?

Answer: State that borders Washington to the east

QUESTION: What is Idaho?

Answer: Country that borders Washington to the north

QUESTION: What is Canada?

Answer: River that forms the border between Washington and Oregon

QUESTION: What is the Columbia River?

Answer: Ocean found on Washington's western edge

QUESTION: What is the Pacific Ocean?

Hurry! I'm next.

Washington
This Land is Our Land

Answer: Washington's tallest mountain

QUESTION: What is Mount Rainier?

Answer: Washington's largest natural lake

QUESTION: What is Lake Chelan?

Answer: Largest manmade lake in Washington

QUESTION: What is Franklin D. Roosevelt Lake?

Answer: Arm of the Pacific Ocean that extends from Admiralty Inlet to Olympia

QUESTION: What is Puget Sound?

Answer: International waterway between British Columbia and Washington

QUESTION: What is the Strait of Juan de Fuca?

Washington
Early Days

Answer: Native American tribal leaders on Washington's coast hosted these incredible parties to show off their wealth, which many times left them nearly penniless.

QUESTION: What are potlatches?

Answer: Indian language used by Washington's tribal groups when trading with each other

QUESTION: What is Chinook?

Answer: He was the first American to arrive in the Pacific Northwest in 1792, and he named the Columbia River.

QUESTION: Who was Robert Gray?

Answer: British explorer who mapped the Washington coast and who named the Puget Sound, Whidbey Island, and more

QUESTION: Who was George Vancouver?

Answer: They were the leaders of the expedition sent by President Thomas Jefferson to explore the lands bought with the Louisiana Purchase in 1803.

QUESTION: Who were Meriwether Lewis and William Clark?

Hey! Where you goin'?

To the next page!

Washington
Patriotic People

Answer: Walla Walla-born general who led the defense at Bataan and Corregidor until forced to surrender during World War II

QUESTION: Who is Jonathan Mayhew Wainwright?

Answer: Washington politician who served as U.S. representative, U.S. senator, and as the U.S. secretary of transportation under President Jimmy Carter

QUESTION: Who was Brock Adams?

Answer: He served as mayor of Seattle and as U.S. secretary of the interior under President William Taft.

QUESTION: Who was Richard Achilles Ballinger?

Answer: He served the longest term in history as an associate justice on the U.S. Supreme Court from 1939–1975.

QUESTION: Who was William O. Douglas?

Answer: She served as chairman of the U.S. Atomic Energy Commission under President Richard Nixon and was Washington's first woman governor.

QUESTION: Who was Dixy Lee Ray?

Washington
Conflicts and Hostilities

Answer: The massacre of Marcus and Narcissa Whitman and 12 others marked the beginning of this Indian war in 1847.

QUESTION: What was the Cayuse War?

Answer: War between the United States and Great Britain was almost the result when an American shot an Englishman's pig on San Juan Island in 1859.

QUESTION: What was the Pig War?

Answer: Washington workers produced airplanes, ships, and aluminum used during this war.

QUESTION: What was World War II?

Answer: Tacoma Army base built during World War I

QUESTION: What is Fort Lewis?

Answer: More than 60,000 workers walked off their jobs in this 1919 event which was the nation's first general strike.

QUESTION: What was the Seattle Revolution of 1919?

Washington
Real Estate

Answer: Puget Sound port city that is Washington's largest city

QUESTION: What is Seattle?

Answer: Area of Washington that lies between the Pacific Ocean, Puget Sound, and the Strait of Juan de Fuca

QUESTION: What is the Olympic Peninsula?

Answer: Mountain range that divides Washington into two different weather regions

QUESTION: What are the Cascades?

Answer: Name given to the part of Washington that lies east of the Cascades

QUESTION: What is the Inland Empire?

Answer: Largest city in eastern Washington

QUESTION: What is Spokane?

It's great to be home again.

Yeah!

Washington
A Date To Remember

Monday	Tuesday	Wednesday	Thursday	Friday	Saturday	Sunday
		1	2	3	4	5

Answer: In 1836, they founded an Indian mission near present-day Walla Walla.

QUESTION: Who were Marcus and Narcissa Whitman?

Answer: In 1853, Congress created this territory which included present-day Washington, northern Idaho, and western Montana.

QUESTION: What was Washington Territory

Answer: In 1846, a treaty between the United States and Great Britain set the boundary between Washington and this country at the 49th parallel.

QUESTION: What is Canada?

Answer: The year Washington became a state

QUESTION: What is 1889?

Answer: Washington volcano that erupted in 1980

QUESTION: What is Mount St. Helens?

Got a date?

Can't be late!

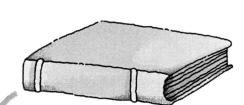

Washington
Scholarly Smarts

Answer: The state office that supervises Washington's public school system

QUESTION: What is the Office of the State Superintendent of Public Instruction?

Answer: Hudson's Bay Company opened the first school in Washington for its employees here in 1832.

QUESTION: What was Fort Vancouver?

Answer: State university located in Seattle that was founded in 1861

QUESTION: What is the University of Washington?

Answer: State university founded in Pullman in 1890

QUESTION: What is Washington State University?

Answer: Walla Walla college originally established as Whitman Seminary in 1859 in memory of Marcus and Narcissa Whitman

QUESTION: What is Whitman College?

Washington
First and Foremost

Answer: Sonora Louise Smart Dodd came up with idea for this special day and the first one was held in Spokane on June 19, 1910.

QUESTION: What is Father's Day?

Answer: John Jacob Astor's Pacific Fur Company established the first American settlement in Washington here.

QUESTION: What is Fort Okanogan?

Answer: The first of these at Hanford began operation in 1944.

QUESTION: What are reactors?

Answer: Construction on one of the first roads built in Washington began in 1859 and covered 624 miles (1,004 kilometers) from Fort Benton, Montana, to Fort Walla Walla, Washington.

QUESTION: What was the Mullan Road?

Answer: Washington's first apple tree was planted here in 1826.

We're number one!

QUESTION: What was Fort Vancouver?

Grown in
Washington

Answer: Washington is the nation's leading producer of this fruit.

QUESTION: What are apples?

Answer: The two varieties of apples Washington is most famous for

QUESTION: What are Red Delicious and Golden Delicious?

Answer: Grain that is Washington's number one crop

QUESTION: What is wheat?

Answer: Washington is a leader in the production of this red berry.

QUESTION: What is the red raspberry?

Answer: Underground plant parts grown in Washington that produce lilies, irises, and tulips

QUESTION: What are flower bulbs?

Did you see that?

Washington
Music and Film

Answer: Tacoma-born singer and actor whose best-selling record was "White Christmas" and who won an Academy Award for best actor

QUESTION: Who was Bing Crosby?

Answer: Seattle musician and composer known for his guitar playing and the songs "Purple Haze" and "Hey, Joe"

QUESTION: Who was Jimi Hendrix?

Answer: Spokane actor who has appeared in the television series *Coach* and *The District* and in the film *Poltergeist*

QUESTION: Who is Craig T. Nelson?

Answer: Walla Walla actor best known for his role in the television series *Batman*

QUESTION: Who is Adam West?

Answer: Television personality born in Darrington who has been the long-time host of game show *The Price is Right*

QUESTION: Who is Bob Barker?

Ready for your 15 minutes?

Yeah!

Answer: Built for the 1962 World's Fair, this has become a symbol for the city of Seattle.

QUESTION: What is the Space Needle?

Answer: Found on the Snake River in southeastern Washington, it is the deepest canyon in the continental United States.

QUESTION: What is Hells Canyon?

Answer: Waterfalls found in eastern Washington that drop 185 feet (56 meters) over a basalt rim of the Columbia Plateau

QUESTION: What are the Palouse Falls?

Answer: One of the most photographed spots in the state is Picture Lake and the mountain reflected in the water.

QUESTION: What is Mount Shuskan?

Answer: Found in the Columbia River Gorge, this 840-foot (256-meter) rock is what remains of a volcano core that was a sign to travelers passing through the Cascade Rapids.

QUESTION: What is Beacon Rock?

Washington
Weather or Not

Answer: Part of Washington that has mild, wet winters and cool summers

QUESTION: What is western Washington?

Answer: Part of Washington that is driest and has cold winters and hot summers

QUESTION: What is eastern Washington?

Answer: The record for the most snow recorded in one year on this Washington mountain is 1,124 inches (2,855 centimeters).

QUESTION: What is Mount Baker?

Answer: Washington mountain that holds the world record for the most snow in a single month at 25 feet, 5 inches (7.7 meters)

QUESTION: What is Mount Rainier?

Answer: Washington mountain range that gets 140 inches (356 centimeters) of precipitation each year

QUESTION: What are the Olympic Mountains?

Washington
Scavenger Hunt

Answer: Found near Blaine, this six-story arch on the U.S./Canadian border commemorates the countries' friendship.

QUESTION: What is Peace Arch State Park?

Answer: The longest, unbroken lava tube cave in the Western Hemisphere is found on the south side of Mount St. Helens.

QUESTION: What is Ape Cave?

Answer: Found in Maryhill, this memorial to soldiers who died in World War I resembles its namesake found in England's Salisbury Plain.

QUESTION: What is Stonehenge?

Answer: Built in 1856, this Ilwaco lighthouse is the oldest in the Pacific Northwest.

QUESTION: What is Cape Disappointment Lighthouse?

Answer: Bellingham house built in 1856 for the general who later led the Confederate charge at the Battle of Gettysburg

QUESTION: What is the George E. Pickett House?

Answer: Mead park that is home to more than two dozen big cats

QUESTION: What is the Cat Tales Endangered Species Conservation Park?

Answer: Sequim location that is home to exotic animals that have retired from show business

QUESTION: What is the Olympic Game Farm?

Answer: Outstanding natural attractions are found at this Seattle zoo.

QUESTION: What is the Woodland Park Zoo?

Answer: Washington's tallest lighthouse at 107 feet (33 meters) was built here in 1898.

QUESTION: What is Westport?

Answer: Tacoma park that is home to a zoo, an aquarium, and a replica of Fort Nisqually

QUESTION: What is Point Defiance?

Washington
Counties

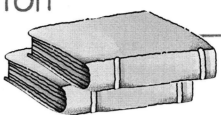

Answer: The number of counties in Washington

QUESTION: What is 39?

Answer: Washington's most populated county

QUESTION: What is King County?

Answer: Washington's largest county

QUESTION: What is Okanogan County?

Answer: Three-member boards that govern most of Washington's counties

QUESTION: What is a board of commissioners?

Answer: County that is composed entirely of islands

QUESTION: What is Island County?

Washington
Creeping Critters

Answer: Fish that leave the salt water and struggle against rapids to get to freshwater to lay their eggs

QUESTION: What are salmon?

Answer: Herds of Roosevelt, or Olympic, elk, the largest members of the deer family, can be found here.

QUESTION: What is the Olympic Peninsula?

Answer: Both the Rocky Mountain and California species of this animal are found in Washington's mountains.

QUESTION: What are bighorn sheep?

Answer: Largest of the toothed whales found living in pods in Washington's inland waters

QUESTION: What are killer, or orca, whales?

Answer: Cat-like animal, also known as a lynx, found in the Paysaten Wilderness high country in northeastern Washington

QUESTION: What is a bobcat?

Washington
Indian Powwow

Answer: Rock paintings made by early Native Americans found on cliffsides

QUESTION: What are pictographs?

Answer: Drawings carved into rock by ancient Native Americans

QUESTION: What are petroglyphs?

Answer: Yakima chief who led his people during the Indian Wars of 1855–1858

QUESTION: Who was Kamiakin?

Answer: The city of Seattle is named for this chief of Puget Sound tribes who remained loyal to settlers during the Indian Wars.

QUESTION: Who was Seathl?

Answer: Spokane Indian chief who started one of the first Indian schools and who maintained friendly relations with settlers

QUESTION: Who was Spokane Garry?

Washington
Prestigious Politics

Answer: Person who heads the executive branch of the state government

QUESTION: Who is the governor?

Answer: Branch of state government that includes the courts

QUESTION: What is the judicial branch?

Answer: The number of years in the term served by governors and state senators

QUESTION: What are four years?

Answer: Branch of state government that makes laws

QUESTION: What is the legislative branch?

Answer: Branch of state government that carries out the laws

QUESTION: What is the executive branch?

Do you think I'll win?

It could happen.

Washington
Lofty Leaders

Answer: Washington politician who was first elected as U.S. representative in 1965 and was named speaker of the house in 1989

QUESTION: Who was Thomas Stephen Foley?

Answer: Mayor of Seattle from 1926–1928, she was the first woman elected as mayor of a large U.S. city.

QUESTION: Who was Bertha Knight Landes?

Answer: Washington's first Chinese-American governor, he was elected in 1996.

QUESTION: Who is Gary Locke?

Answer: He served Washington as a U.S. representative and senator and ran unsuccessfully for president in 1972 and 1976.

QUESTION: Who was Henry "Scoop" Jackson?

Answer: First territorial governor of Washington

QUESTION: Who was Isaac Ingalls Stevens?

Washington
Statehood

Answer: The date Washington became a state

QUESTION: What is November 11, 1889?

Answer: Washington's state capital

QUESTION: What is Olympia?

Answer: He was elected as Washington's first governor.

QUESTION: Who was Elisha P. Ferry?

Answer: He was the U.S. president who signed the law making Washington a state

QUESTION: Who was President Benjamin Harrison?

Answer: Document approved by Washington Territory voters, then sent to Washington, D.C., for approval before Washington became a state

QUESTION: What is the state constitution?

Answer: He founded Microsoft, the world's largest computer software company that is headquartered in Redmond.

QUESTION: Who is Bill Gates?

Answer: She was the first woman to climb Mount Rainier.

QUESTION: Who was Fay Fuller?

Answer: News reporter who is considered the "Father of Television News"

QUESTION: Who was Edmund R. Murrow?

Answer: Seattle-born dancer-choreographer who founded the Joffrey Ballet

QUESTION: Who was Robert Joffrey?

Answer: Tacoma cartoonist who created *The Far Side*

QUESTION: Who is Gary Larson?

Washington
Flag Facts

Answer: Year the state flag was adopted by the legislature

QUESTION: What was 1923?

Answer: The color of the state flag's field

QUESTION: What is green?

Answer: The design found in the center of the state flag

QUESTION: What is the state seal?

Answer: The person whose likeness appears on the state flag

QUESTION: Who was George Washington?

Answer: The Olympia jeweler who designed the state seal in 1889

Which way do we go?

West! I think.

QUESTION: Who was Charles Talcott?

Washington
Arts & Artists

Answer: Artist who drew the only surviving portraits of Indian chiefs in the Columbia River region

QUESTION: Who was Gustav Sohon?

Answer: Pianist who opened the Cornish College of the Arts in Seattle

QUESTION: Who was Nellie Cornish?

Answer: Sculptor who has won acclaim for his fountains

QUESTION: Who is George Tsutakawa?

Answer: Sculptor who makes shell-like shapes out of glass

QUESTION: Who is Dale Chihuly?

Answer: His work features historic scenes of African-American leaders such as Frederick Douglass and Harriet Tubman.

QUESTION: Who is Jacob Lawrence?

Washington
Big on Basics

Answer: Former slave who founded Centralia

QUESTION: Who was George Washington?

Answer: Hudson's Bay Company employee who built Fort Vancouver on the Columbia River in 1825

QUESTION: Who was John McLoughlin?

Answer: Spokane boardinghouse owner and millionaire who was a leader of women's suffrage in Washington

QUESTION: Who was Mary Awkwright Hutton?

Answer: In the late 1890s and early 1900s, Seattle became the main supply center for the gold rush in this location.

QUESTION: What is Alaska (or the Klondike)?

Answer: When settlers first started coming to Washington, it was considered part of this.

QUESTION: What is Oregon Country?

Washington
Literary Laureates

Answer: Hoquiam-born writer best known for *Gentle Ben*, *Year of the Black Pony*, and *Scrub Dog of Alaska*

QUESTION: Who was Walt Morey?

Answer: Using another name, Jessie Mercer Payzant wrote 38 children's books including *Saucer in the Sea*, *Kidlik's Kayak*, and *A Trip to Mexico*.

QUESTION: Who is Terry Shannon?

Answer: Also known as Mrs. Joseph Auslander, she won a Pulitzer Prize for poetry in 1953 for *Bright Ambush.*

QUESTION: Who was Audrey May Wurdemann?

Answer: Seattle-born author who wrote under 20 different pen names, including Max Brand and Evan Evans

QUESTION: Who was Frederick Faust?

Answer: A science fiction writer, he is the author of the Dune series.

QUESTION: Who is Frank Herbert?

Washington
Natural Resources

Answer: Washington is the only western state with large deposits of this fuel found in the western part of the state.

QUESTION: What is coal?

Answer: Salmon is the most prized catch in this Washington industry.

QUESTION: What is fishing?

Answer: Washington is second in the nation in the production of this.

QUESTION: What is lumber?

Answer: It is the most abundant tree species found in Washington.

QUESTION: What is Douglas fir?

Answer: Half of Washington state is covered with these.

QUESTION: What are forests?

Washington

From A to Z

Answer: Washington's state gem

QUESTION: What is petrified wood?

Answer: Washington's state fruit

QUESTION: What is the apple?

Answer: Washington's state fossil

QUESTION: What is the Columbia mammoth?

Answer: Washington's state insect

QUESTION: What is the green darner dragonfly?

Answer: Washington's state grass

QUESTION: What is bluebunch wheatgrass?

Well— here we are.

Yeah!